El primer cuerpo de bomberos

por Jane Simon
ilustrado por Joe Kulka

HOUGHTON MIFFLIN   BOSTON

Hace mucho tiempo, los incendios representaban un gran peligro para la gente que vivía en nuestro país.

En esos tiempos, la gente vivía en casas de madera. Tenían chimeneas encendidas para calentar la casa y para cocinar. También prendían velas para ver en la noche.

A veces se incendiaban las casas de madera.

Pero no existían los bomberos.

Todas las familias tenían un balde colgado en la puerta del frente. Cuando empezaba el fuego los llenaban de agua y trataban de apagar el fuego.

Pero la madera arde rápidamente. Muchas veces, los edificios se quemaban completamente antes de que se lograra apagar el fuego.

Los incendios causaban muchos daños en las ciudades grandes. Allí las casas de madera estaban unas junto a otras.

8

Ben Franklin vivía en una ciudad en la que había muchos incendios.

Ben escribió sobre los incendios en el periódico. Poco después, treinta personas lo ayudaron a formar el primer cuerpo de bomberos.

Los bomberos tenían coches de bombas sencillos y mangueras. Tenían que bombear el agua a mano.

Pero consiguieron apagar muchos incendios. Desde entonces, los bomberos han hecho de nuestros pueblos y ciudades lugares más seguros para vivir.

Guide Notes

Title: Marvelous Menus
Stage: Fluency (2)

Text Form: Menus
Approach: Guided Reading
Processes: Thinking Critically, Exploring Language, Processing Information
Written and Visual Focus: Menus, Signs

THINKING CRITICALLY
(sample questions)
- If you were at the Rodents' Restaurant, what would you think was meant by the words "manager's special"?
- Why do you think you can get packaged meals from the Tigers' Takeaways?
- What do you think is meant by the words "No-wait meals"?
- What sort of things do you think you would find at a dessert bar?

EXPLORING LANGUAGE

Terminology
Spread, author and illustrator credits, ISBN number

Vocabulary
Clarify: combo, grilled, wedges, barrow, manager
Nouns: meals, burgers, menu, dessert
Verbs: cook, run, fry, bake
Singular/plural: drink/drinks, nut/nuts, fish/fish

Print Conventions
Dash, apostrophe – possessive (Cats' Cafe, Dinosaurs' Dial-a-meal, Dragons' Diner)
Parenthesis: (all light meals), (with raisins)

Phonological Patterns
Focus on short and long vowel **i** (b**i**scuits, f**i**sh, r**i**bs, **i**ce cream, w**i**ld)
Discuss root words – topped, sizzling
Look at suffix **y** (crisp**y**, cream**y**, meat**y**, tast**y**)

Step Three
Look at your list of foods. Put the dishes under the right heading.

MENU
Breakfast
Pancakes
Lunch
Pizza
Fruit salad
Dinner
Roast chicken
Fish and fries
Spaghetti
Apple pie

(You could also write how much each dish will cost.)

Step Four
Now you could write a short description for each dish. You could say what is in the dish and how it tastes.

MENU
Breakfast
Pancakes filled with berries-very sweet
Lunch
Pizza with tomato and mushroom – delicious

Remember: You can use interesting letters and designs to make your menu look great!

Food Menus

Purpose: to list and describe food dishes

How to Write a Food Menu:

Step One
Think about the foods you want on your menu. Make a list of the foods.

> Pizza
> Fruit salad
> Roast chicken
> Pancakes
> Fish and fries
> Spaghetti
> Apple pie

Step Two
Decide what headings your menu will have. You could start with:
Breakfast
Lunch
Dinner

Or you could choose headings such as:
Starters
Mains
Desserts
Drinks

DOGS' DRIVE-THROUGH

No-wait Meals $3.00

Big Bone Barbecue
A healthy choice for those on the run. Big bones cooked until tender with gravy and a salad of your choice.

Smoked Ribs
Smoked ribs with a wild berry sauce

Cat's Tail Soup
Good after a hard day's work!

Munchie Crunchies
Meat biscuits baked till hard. Good for the teeth!

Burgers
Burgers served with cheese, lettuce, and tomato

Drinks $1.00

Soda pop with ice cream
Soda pop with lime ice

Wild Cow
Hot milk with cream topping

Elephants' Eatery

Salad Barrow

$5.00 for a wheelbarrow

Lettuce, cabbages, carrots, apples, turnips, nuts, seeds, and corn

Cooked Food

$4.00 a bucket

Cabbage Stew with sauce made from orange juice

Veggie Delights
Spinach and broccoli with herbs and squashed tomatoes

Desserts
$3.00 a barrel

Apples

Pears

Buns (with raisins)

DRAGONS' DINER

Hot Sandwiches

Toast Your Own Sandwiches
(You add the fire – two minutes each side.)

Red Hot Snacks on wheat bread:

Smokey Tail

Sizzling Snake Fangs

Chili Mice

Bats' Tails

All $2.50

Delicious Desserts
$1.00

Bat Wing Pudding
A special dessert (warmed by dragon fire) with hot toffee on top

High Flying Moonlight Pie
with delicious slime

Cave Crumble
A family favorite with crunchy rock topping

TIGER TAKEAWAYS

Packaged Meals

Pack One:
Chicken Stew
Pot roasted, tender and tasty meat in gravy

Pack Two:
Rabbit Pie
Rabbit with baked potatoes and fresh salad

Pack Three:
Goat on the Hoof
Baked in a wood oven

Packs $5.00 each

Extras

Golden wedges
Fried mushrooms
Onion rings
Corn

All 50 cents a tub

Drinks

Lion's Roar
Lemonade and soda

Cheetah Chase
Lime with lots of ice

Drinks $1.00 each

DINOSAURS' DIAL - A - MEAL

Pizza

Small $15.00
Medium $18.00
Large $20.00

T-Rex Combo
T-Rex meaty strips with onions and cheese

Pizza to Go
A crispy pizza with swamp greens, moss, and sweet leaves

Desserts

Pterosaur Pie
A sweet creamy cake with roasted nuts

Tyrannosaur Cake
Cheesecake topped with slime from local caves

(All desserts $3.00)

MAY OFFER 10% OFF ALL MEALS

CATS' CAFE

Afternoon Snacks

Snack for One $2.50

Snack for Two $2.25 ea.

Snack for Three $2.00 ea.

Coffee and Fish Cakes $3.00

Sandwiches

Fish sandwiches on wheat bread $2.00

Toasted, add 50 cents

Light Meals

Meaty Bites with sour cream

Grilled Fish Balls with sauce

Mouse Pie with green peas

Shrimp and Fish Salad with tomato

Pizza topped with tuna and cheese

(All Light Meals $8.95)

Desserts

Choose from our Dessert Bar $2.00

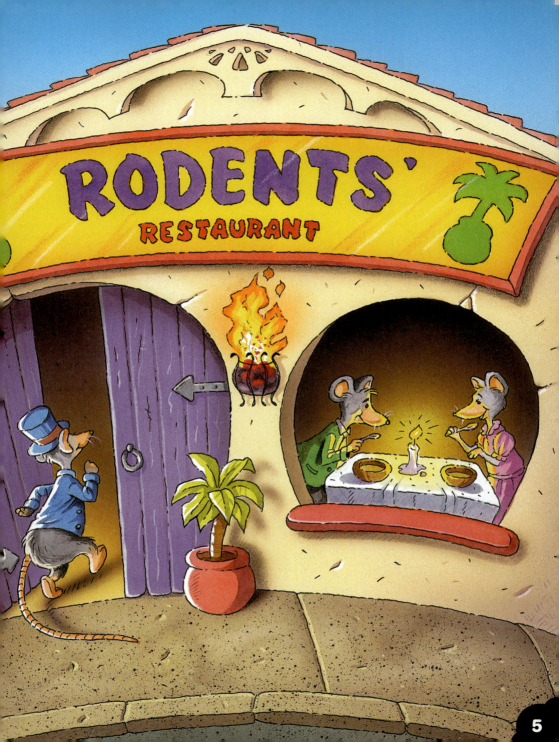

RODENTS' RESTAURANT
FINE DINING

Starters
Grass Seeds $4.95

Field Salad $4.50

Soup
Soup of the Day:
Mouse Nest Soup
$3.75

Mains
Cat Tail Stew $13.50
Tails cooked
in fresh herbs

Cheese Delight $15.90
Cheese balls served
with mushrooms

Manager's Special
Grilled Nuts $13.00
Nuts wrapped in leaves
with a hot sauce

Desserts
Beady Eye
Delight $7.95
Four scoops of ice
cream sprinkled with
roasted nuts

Whisker's
Surprise $4.95
Bread pudding with a
butter sauce